Original title:
A Paradise of Your Own

Copyright © 2025 Creative Arts Management OÜ
All rights reserved.

Author: Maxwell Donovan
ISBN HARDBACK: 978-1-80581-491-7
ISBN PAPERBACK: 978-1-80581-018-6
ISBN EBOOK: 978-1-80581-491-7

Where Cloud Meets Soil

A cloud with legs, so goofy and round,
Dances on fields, making silly sounds.
With rain that tickles the flowers' bright faces,
They laugh together in silly embraces.

Butterflies join in with a hop and a spin,
While worms in the dirt have a giggle within.
Frogs croak in rhythm, a quirky delight,
As nature's odd circus performs through the night.

Fictional Greenery

Trees wearing hats, quite stylish and grand,
Giggle at squirrels who can't understand.
The grass is a carpet of jellybean hues,
Where dandelions whisper their cheeky news.

Sunflowers chat with the butterflies bright,
Trading their secrets in day and in night.
The brook tells tall tales, with splashes and churns,
While rocks roll their eyes at the lesson that burns.

Cradle of Calm

In a cradle of calm, where giggles abound,
Laughter's the music, the softest of sounds.
Clouds on a swing set, they sway and they sway,
Telling tall tales of their floaty ballet.

The sun plays peekaboo, hiding with glee,
While a lazy cat naps on the shade of a tree.
Time takes a break, it slips through the cracks,
As happiness skips along funny little tracks.

Eden's Secret

In Eden's secret, a place full of cheer,
Giggling goldfish swim, they have no fear.
Trees with candy, berries made of dreams,
Where everything's funny, or so it seems.

The breeze tells jokes, making flowers all shake,
And the moon chuckles, causing ripples in lakes.
It's a place where fun grows on brightly green vines,
And laughter's the nectar that everyone finds.

The Meadow of Your Making

In a meadow filled with clover,
Bumblebees dance and hover.
A squirrel wears a tiny hat,
I think he's quite the chatty brat.

With daisies sprouting everywhere,
I tripped and landed in a chair.
A rabbit laughed, then ran away,
Maybe he'll join my next ballet.

The butterflies are having fun,
Spreading gossip in the sun.
While ants march in a grand parade,
They think they're fierce, but I'll invade!

So here I'll twirl and spin about,
In my meadow, I won't pout.
With giggles sprinkled in the air,
My fun-filled world is free of care.

The Island of Serene Reflections

On my island made of jelly,
Even turtles groove and belly.
Seagulls wear sunglasses so bright,
Throwing shade with all their might.

Palm trees sway like dancers bold,
With coconuts that don't grow old.
The waves sing songs of silly tunes,
As crabs do the twist under the moons.

The sun sets in a goofy way,
Painting everything in disarray.
I sip my drink and spot a fish,
It offered me a birthday wish!

With laughter echoing through the night,
My island dreams are pure delight.
Surrounded by humor so profound,
In this haven, joy is found.

Arbors of Personal Bliss

Under the trees, I sip my drink,
Finding shade, it's time to think.
Critters dance, on toes so small,
I giggle loud, they start to fall.

A squirrel steals my tasty snack,
I chase it down, but it won't crack.
In this grove, life's a fun race,
Who knew peace brought such a face?

The Canvas of Inner Meadows

On grassy plains, I trip and roll,
Painting my dreams, with a silly goal.
Butterflies laugh as they flutter by,
While I tumble, oh my, oh my!

A cow paints smiles with its moo,
Grazing calm, just like me too.
Each brush stroke whispers a joke,
As laughter blooms with every poke.

A Voyage Through Tranquil Thoughts

On a raft of giggles, I float along,
Paddling softly to a silly song.
Fish splash around, they wave and cheer,
While I try to keep dry, oh dear!

Each thought's a wave, they crash with flair,
Making me laugh, as I breathe fresh air.
A turtle points with its tiny nail,
"Perhaps try the ship—it's a better sail!"

Hues of Freedom's Embrace

With crayons bright, I scribble free,
A rainbow squirrel perched on a tree.
Colors clash, they dance and pop,
In my world, there's never a stop.

The sun wears shades, it winks at me,
Saying, "Life's a joke, just wait and see!"
Clouds tickle the sky with fluff and cheer,
As I color outside each line, my dear!

Pathways to Inner Radiance

In a garden where socks grow free,
Even the bees wear tie-dye, you see.
A tree that shakes out jellybeans,
And squirrels write songs about jelly queens.

A trampoline hill in the sun,
Where laughter's the only way to run.
Chasing rainbows on pogo sticks,
Happiness is playing silly tricks.

The Refuge of Sweet Solace

In a hammock made from spaghetti strands,
I sip sunshine and build pudding lands.
Where flip-flops become tiny boats,
And jellyfish wear cute little coats.

Bubbles float while the stars come down,
And unicorns use ice cream for a crown.
Here, the giggles never cease,
And nonsense reigns, granting feathery peace.

A Tapestry of Forgotten Dreams

In a closet of mismatched shoes,
Lies a world where no one snooze.
Hats dance on heads of floating cats,
And the clocks tick backwards, how 'bout that?

Each dream is a sandwich, thick and wide,
Filled with laughter, and pickle pride.
Here, nap time means playtime instead,
As marshmallow clouds cradle your head.

The Well of Untold Stories

Down by a well that sings of pie,
Fish tell tales of their dreams to fly.
The laughter spills like raindrops clear,
While spaghetti monsters have no fear.

Beneath the twinkling, wiggly stars,
Chickens moonwalk and dance with cars.
To soak in joy's eccentric glow,
We swim in stories, let our quirks flow.

Places Untold.

In a garden of lost socks, I play,
Where mismatched pairs come out to sway.
Sunflowers joke with the tulips bright,
As bunnies hop in the golden light.

A treehouse built with Lego blocks,
Hosts tea parties for giggling flocks.
The clouds wear hats, the sun has shades,
And butterflies dance in quirky parades.

In this land of giggles and cheer,
Silly sprinkles rain down from near.
Dancing shoelaces spin in delight,
As shadows laugh at the silly sight.

So come take a seat on the lumpy ground,
Where silly whispers are all around.
In places untold, let your soul be free,
In the comical world of whimsy we see.

Whispers of a Secret Haven

In the nook where llamas wear bow ties,
And kiwi birds take the night skies.
A pickle jar glows with giggles and glee,
Telling secrets of socks that run wild and free.

The ice cream cones stand proudly tall,
While cherries compete in a friendly brawl.
Jellybeans tumble down the hill,
Leaving trails of laughter, a sweet thrill.

The bushes gossip, they know all the lore,
Of dancing cats and a candy store.
In whispers soft as the moonbeams glow,
They hold the secrets of this fun show.

Here, in this haven, the silly abound,
With giggles and snorts as the daily sound.
Join in the fun, it's where laughter's born,
In this whispering land, each dawn reborn.

When Dreams Find Their Nest

When dreams gather 'round for a pajama bash,
They sip on fizzy drinks and make a splash.
Cuddly bears play hopscotch, you see,
As stars giggle down from a green gum tree.

Silly hats made of rainbow fluff,
Everyone's smiling, it's never too tough.
Cheese wheels roll down like bouncy balls,
And jellyfish join in with whimsical calls.

In this dreamy spot, no worries reside,
Just cupcake clouds and a marshmallow slide.
A jellybean tide washes stress away,
While happy thoughts come out to play.

When dreams find a nest, we dance through the night,
Under the moon, everything feels right.
So let your giggles soar high in the air,
In this land where fun is beyond compare.

Sanctuary of Solitude

In the quiet corner of my cozy space,
A sanctuary filled with an odd embrace.
Cats in pajamas lounge on the floor,
As donuts hang out and plan to explore.

The walls are painted in colors of cheese,
And sunlight spills through with the greatest of ease.
My slippers tell stories of adventures bold,
While pillows whisper secrets yet untold.

Here, solitude wears a whimsical hat,
In the company of giggles and a chatty cat.
A teapot croons a delightful tune,
As funny tales dance around like a balloon.

In this quirky nook, I take a repose,
Among wild laughter and silly prose.
In the sanctuary, every odd thought can roam,
In this quirky haven, I find my true home.

Heartstring Haven

In a land where socks are never lost,
And ice cream flows like rivers tossed.
Cats wear hats and dogs can speak,
Every day's a funny peak.

A tree that giggles when you climb,
And clouds that dance to silly rhyme.
Take a nap on trampoline chairs,
With rubber ducks for all your cares.

Your fridge is filled with candy dreams,
Where laughter bubbles, or so it seems.
A place where pranks are all the rage,
And time is but a laughing page.

Gardens of the Imagination

In gardens where the wild things grow,
Turtles wear tuxedos, don't you know?
Flowers speak in rhymes so bright,
While fairies dance with wigs of light.

Bunnies bake a carrot cake,
While frogs play hopscotch by the lake.
Sunflowers wear their best attire,
Each gossiping like they conspire.

Butterflies with polka dots,
Flap about and tie up knots.
Rain falls up, and pigs can fly,
In this place, you'd never sigh.

Spheres of Peace

In spheres so round where giggles swell,
Floating on clouds like jelly bell.
Everyone wears mismatched shoes,
While sipping lemonade infused with blues.

Hammocks swaying in mid-air,
Hosting parties without a care.
Chickens play chess, oh what a sight!
They peck at pawns till the stars ignite.

The sun is shy, it hides behind
Pancake hills for you to find.
With laughter echoing near and far,
You'll spot a hedgehog driving a car.

Echoes of Elysium

In echo lands where giggles ring,
Ducks juggle balls, it's quite the fling.
Here, rainbows slide like ribbons wide,
While moonbeams play and kittens hide.

Giant marshmallows dot the shore,
As jelly beans knock on your door.
Echoes of laughter bounce around,
In this space, joy can be found.

Elephants dance on roller skates,
The sun juggles pies with gracious fates.
With wiggles and wobbles, good times flow,
In this realm where the fun will grow.

Escape to Reverie

In a land of socks that never lose,
A breeze of laughter, not a snooze.
With marshmallow clouds, oh so high,
We dance with squirrels, oh my, oh my!

The sun wears shades, a sunny chap,
While rainbows play a silly map.
We surf on waves of jellybeans,
And ride our bikes on candy scenes.

An old tree whispers jokes galore,
While owls hoot tales of yore.
Tickling grass and giggling trees,
In a world where no one says please.

Join me there, where whimsy's root,
Grows flowers that play the kazoo flute.
With every step, a giggle blooms,
In this land of colorful whims!

The Place You Create

In a room where shadows toss and play,
Monkeys serve tea in a grand ballet.
A cat in a hat tells jokes so neat,
And shoes that dance on tiny feet.

Walls made of chocolate, sweet delight,
Cuddle up with pillows, soft and tight.
Each corner filled with giggling sound,
In every knickknack, joy is found.

Bubbles float by like silly dreams,
While the floor is covered in whipped cream.
We ride on chairs that fly through space,
In the perfect, cozy laughing place.

Bring along your silliest grin,
For in this realm, we all can win.
With every laugh, the hours fade,
In the world we whimsically made!

Enchanted Retreat

In a forest where trees wear crowns so bright,
The flowers play tags, what a sight!
A river giggles as it flows along,
Singing silly tunes, a joyful song.

Frogs in tuxedos hop around,
While butterflies twirl on merry ground.
Pizza trees, with toppings galore,
Make every meal a fun encore.

Clouds of glitter drift so high,
As we catch dreams that float by.
Friendly trolls invite us to dance,
In the glow of a rainbow's chance.

So gather 'round, let laughter ring,
In this retreat where joy's the king.
With every step, the mood aligns,
In the land of jokes and doodle designs!

Haven of Colors

Here in a town of polka dot skies,
Gummy bears wear big surprise ties.
Kite-flying goats race the bright sun,
Laughing together, oh what fun!

Cupcakes grow large on candy cane trees,
While pickle juice flows with the breeze.
Jellyfish juggle on trampoline mats,
Silly adventures with goofy spats.

Every road sings a merry tune,
As marshmallow moons dance with the dune.
The paint drips joy in every hue,
Creating a masterpiece just for you.

So come on down to this colorful cheer,
Where laughter bursts like bright chandeliers.
In this haven of mirth and spree,
Joy is abundant, come play with me!

Notes of Stillness

In a hammock where I sway,
With a sloth who's lost his way,
We giggle at the clouds above,
While counting birds who don't get love.

The spiders weave their sticky art,
I wonder if they have a chart,
To show the routes of flies that roam,
And find a cozy place called home.

The breeze confides in whisper tone,
While ants march like they own the throne,
I laugh, they dance, it's quite a show,
In my own world where time moves slow.

How sweet it is to just unwind,
With these odd pals who are so kind,
To make this space a silly fest,
Here's where I feel my very best.

The Spirit's Sanctuary

In a treehouse made of gum and dreams,
A squirrel sings in silly schemes,
He's planning on a grand buffet,
Of acorns, nuts, and a cabaret.

The stars above wear pajamas bright,
As fireflies laugh and take to flight,
They twirl and spin in a glowing race,
While owls just shake their furry face.

The moon is blue, full of cheese delight,
And wishes sprout like weeds at night,
Join in the fun, oh spirits cheer,
In this sanctuary of good cheer.

The socks from laundry flung on trees,
Are now the flags of gentle breeze,
Who knew that silliness could grow,
In a place where laughter's the flow?

Fantasia in Full Bloom

Underneath the giant flower,
A bee recites a joyful power,
He claims he knows the way to dance,
If only he could find his pants!

The daisies giggle at the show,
While butterflies begin to blow,
Some bubbles filled with honey sweet,
As crickets play their little beat.

The bunnies wear their finest hats,
And join the feast with all the rats,
They have a teacup for a throne,
Where laughter's always brightly shown.

Colors burst and sparkle wide,
In this land where fun won't hide,
So come, my friend, and join the boom,
In this wild and wacky bloom!

Windows to Wonder

Through a window, I can see,
A goldfish that's a big ballet,
He pirouettes through bubbling streams,
And sings as if it's all just dreams.

The flowers gossip, oh so bright,
About the bees who went on strike,
Demanding honey and a ball,
While ants just roll their eyes and crawl.

A cat in shades commands the scene,
Posing like a movie queen,
She flips her tail, oh what a sight,
With dogs who bark of love tonight.

From these windows wide and clear,
I see the world without a fear,
It's filled with laughter, joy, and cheer,
Just look around, my friend, and steer!

The Embrace of Fluttering Leaves

In a world where leaves confide,
Squirrels dance and tiny bugs glide.
The air's a joke, the trees all grin,
Who knew nature could fit in a tin?

The wind whispers secrets and glee,
While laughter bounces off every tree.
Shadows play tag, chasing the sun,
In this leafy realm, all chores are fun!

A bench made of moss, what a chair!
Birds trade gossip without a care.
The grass is a carpet, soft and green,
In this giggly nook, joy is seen!

As twigs tap dance with rhythm and flair,
Every moment's a treasure to share.
If trees can chuckle and rocks can sing,
Then let's all join in this joyful fling!

Together in the Silent Glow

Under a moon with a silly grin,
We knock on dreams, let laughter in.
Stars tell jokes that twinkle bright,
In the hush of night, all feels just right.

Crickets chirp like a wacky band,
Playing tunes in a calm so grand.
The fireflies wink, they're in on the fun,
As we share tales 'til the rising sun.

Clouds drift by wearing cotton candy,
While soft night air feels warm and dandy.
Whispers float like marshmallows sweet,
In this glowing moment, life's a treat!

Together we giggle, together we dream,
In the quiet glow, we're a silly team.
With laughter as fuel, we'll conquer the night,
In this magical nook, all feels just right!

The Perch of Infinite Possibilities

On this branch, our imaginations soar,
With every wobble, we laugh even more.
The world below is a circus parade,
As squirrels sell tickets for shade and lemonade.

Up here, the air is fizzy and light,
Every cloud looks like a fluffy delight.
With dreams like kites, we're set to explore,
In our high-up nest, who could ask for more?

The view's a sketch of mishap and cheer,
Where raindrops dance, and sunlight draws near.
While owls break into a witty debate,
We savor this whimsy, it's simply first-rate!

As branches shake in a playful jest,
We toast to strange things that spark our zest.
From this perch, the world is a show,
Let's laugh at life; let our joy overflow!

The Horizon of Inner Light

With each sunrise, laughter stretches wide,
As giggles greet beams that slip and slide.
The mornings are filled with whirls and twirls,
As sleep takes a bow and excitement unfurls.

Jumbling socks dance on floors of bright hue,
And breakfast is served with a silly view.
Toast hops into butter like a sunny delight,
While jam leads the charge in a tasty fight!

From windows, the world looks like a game,
Where shadows make silly shapes of fame.
Rugs tumble and twirl, welcoming all,
In this light-hearted space, we laugh and sprawl!

So here's to horizons, to mornings so bright,
With laughter as our guide—oh, what a sight!
Let's frolic through life with our hearts full of cheer,
In this canvas of joy, we'll embrace every year!

Shores of Stillness

On the beach where seagulls squawk,
I built a castle from my talk.
The waves laughed while I made a moat,
My dreams drifted out on a float.

With sunscreen smeared upon my nose,
I channeled all those summer woes.
A beach ball bounced, then hit my head,
And all my plans were up and fled.

The crabs performed a lovely dance,
I joined them, giving it a chance.
They pinched my toe, I yelped in glee,
We laughed as one under the tree.

So here I sit with grains of sand,
A goofy smile, a friendly hand.
The day's delight, a silly show,
I found a joy, my heart aglow.

The Heart's Canvas

With paintbrush held in clumsy grip,
I tried to craft a daring trip.
My canvas bloomed in colors bright,
But turned out looking quite a fright.

I splattered red and green all 'round,
The neighbors frowned, I heard them sound.
"Is it a tree or a strange hat?"
My masterpiece a bit of chat.

The dog observed with curious eyes,
As I declared my art the prize.
He barked a laugh, I caught his vibe,
Together we formed the best tribe.

In every stroke, a giggle lived,
Each dribble's tale, my heart just gave.
The colors mixed, my soul did soar,
Creating joy, who could ask for more?

Lullabies of the Lost

In the attic where dust bunnies play,
I found my socks, long gone astray.
A phantom choir sang soft and low,
While I searched for lost treasures to show.

The shadows danced with quite a flair,
They twirled and whirled without a care.
Each step I took, a squeaky floor,
I yawned and laughed, then called for more.

I rocked a chair like a ship at sea,
Imagined a crew who'd sails with me.
We'd navigate through dust and dreams,
And ride the waves with joyful screams.

So off I drifted on waves of sleep,
With funny figures, a secret keep.
Lullabies hummed to my silly quest,
In the attic, I found myself blessed.

Embrace of Illusion

In a world where socks are never paired,
My closet's chaos, I gladly bared.
Each shoe a tale, each shirt a song,
In closets deep where I belong.

The mirror giggled, "Who's that guy?
Your hair's a squiggle, oh me, oh my!"
I practiced poses, made some goofy faces,
While my reflection danced through funny places.

With every blunder, I found delight,
As shadows whispered both day and night.
I wore a hat that looked quite vague,
Toasting joy with my rubber plague.

So come, embrace this wacky ride,
Where laughter's found and fears subside.
In topsy-turvy, we'll find the sun,
In every blip, let's have some fun!

Fields of Infinite Possibility

In fields where grass grows tall and wide,
I trip on roots, my shoes collide.
The daisies laugh, the sun looks down,
As I chase dreams while wearing a frown.

Butterflies wear tiny hats so bold,
While rabbits play cards, if truth be told.
I join their game, I lose my shoe,
In this strange world, I'm feeling new.

Each breeze a whisper, a playful tease,
I've got a ticket for clownish ease.
The flowers nod like pals in jest,
This chaotic bliss is simply the best.

I dance with shadows, I high-five trees,
Who'd think that nature could be such a tease?
With giggles that sway like a joyful song,
In these wild fields, you simply can't go wrong.

The Enchanted Haven

In a nook where the sun spills sweet lemonade,
Ducks wear sunglasses, their coolness displayed.
A squirrel in slippers, he struts with flair,
While lazy cats lounge without a care.

The toys have come to life, it's quite bizarre,
A teddy bear mixes drinks at the bar.
A raucous party with games to play,
A haiku contest? Let's shout hooray!

Magical mushrooms do a jig on the floor,
To the rhythm of laughter, we all ask for more.
A confetti storm of leaves drifts down,
In this haven of giggles, I'll wear my crown.

Unicorns prance and steal the show,
While rainbows help to make puddles grow.
Oh, what a place where silliness reigns,
In this goofy refuge, joy never wanes.

Mirage of Comfort

In a land where socks don't always match,
And every sandwich is a quirky batch.
Pillow forts rise like castles of foam,
As kids rule the day, the whole world their home.

Ice cream flows like rivers of delight,
And sprinkles rain down every day and night.
A cat in a bow tie conducts the band,
As giggling grows louder, isn't it grand?

Each laugh is a cloud drifting high and free,
Bouncing on bubbles, come dance with me!
With nacho trees and a pizza moon,
This mirage of comfort is never too soon.

In a hammock of dreams, we sway and swing,
Under a sky filled with giggles that sing.
Where every corner holds a delightful surprise,
And the sunset turns out to be fries!

Realm of Whimsy

In a realm where the penguins wear bowler hats,
And the chairs debate on which one to chat.
A pencil-drawn dragon holds court on a throne,
While unicorns giggle with candy they've grown.

Cotton candy clouds drift by with flair,
Telling stories of dreams floating in air.
The snails wear capes as they race by the trees,
Yelling, "Wanna bet?" at the funky breeze.

Giggles erupt like fireworks at dusk,
As marshmallow monsters parade in a husk.
With silly hats and mismatched shoes,
Every day here, there's nothing to lose.

A teacup ride spins and spills a bit fun,
With jellybean stars that shine like the sun.
In this whimsical world of laughter and cheer,
Every moment is magic, come join us here!

Blossoms of Imagination

In a garden where ducks wear hats,
Singing songs to the fluffy cats.
Clouds are made of cotton candy,
Irrigation run by folks so dandy.

Chairs that dance and tables sing,
Jellybeans grow from a spring.
Every pet has a joke to tell,
In my mind, it's just swell!

Butterflies sipping soda pop,
Rainbows slide, then suddenly stop.
Trees play chess with the swinging bees,
And the breeze hums sweet melodies.

Pretty wild, this tale I weave,
Who said you can't just believe?
A life where dreams replace the grind,
In my heart, the best unwind.

Retreating to Stillness

A hammock swings between two stars,
While koalas drive tiny cars.
No worries here, just ice cream dreams,
Where everyone giggles and schemes.

Penguin pals, they host a show,
With taps and flips, how they glow!
Forget your tie, wear a tutu,
Fashion's more fun when it's a zoo.

The sun takes naps, the moon plays chess,
While squirrels debate who's the best.
Cats wear glasses, wise and bright,
Who knew daydreams could take flight?

In stillness, we find the curious,
Laughing, we paint our lives delirious.
Take a break, oh what a thrill,
In the moments, time stands still.

Horizon of Hope

Fish wearing boots surf the sea,
Dolphins glitter like confetti.
Sunsets in shades of lemon pie,
Waves that giggle and say goodbye.

Seagulls reading the news aloud,
Coconuts gather a funky crowd.
Every glance paints a smile across,
Wishing we could all just toss!

Turtles share their latest finds,
While crabs attempt their backward grinds.
No one's grumpy, all is bright,
Even the moon gives a wink of light.

Adventure calls from up ahead,
With laughter woven in every thread.
In a world where joy's avowed,
Leap, laugh, don't worry—be proud!

A World of Your Crafting

In this realm of sticky glue,
Llamas wear shoes, oh how they woo!
Pasta plants sway, dancing so bold,
While jellyfish guard hidden gold.

Pancake houses with syrup roofs,
Bouncing toys, watching funny goofs.
Giggles erupt from inside trees,
As squirrels juggle with such ease.

Erase the rules; draw your own fun,
Dig big holes to soak up sun.
Let your crayons run free and wild,
Make it chaotic, be that child!

In this crafting, laughter blooms,
And every corner brightly looms.
Welcome joy with open arms,
Creating magic, raising charms.

Hideaway of the Mind

In a corner, my thoughts take flight,
Where socks dance and laughter ignites.
I build castles from crumbs of my snack,
And invite my daydreams for a chat.

Under the table, my secrets reside,
With a pet rock, my loyal guide.
We whisper jokes about the shoe in the hall,
As we ponder why cats seem to rule all.

A blanket fort stands tall with pride,
In my hideaway where giggles confide.
Monsters all flee for they're scared of the fun,
As I crown myself king of the little one.

Every tickle of chaos brings pure delight,
In this mind maze where silliness takes flight.
So roll me a giggle, let laughter run wild,
In this hideaway, the heart of a child.

Where Wishes Bloom

In a land where socks all mismatch,
And ice-cream rivers lead to a patch.
The trees wear hats, oh what a sight,
While butterflies join in pure delight.

Here, wishes bloom in funny shapes,
Like dancing cats and rhyming grapes.
Jellybeans rain from clouds so bright,
In this world, everything feels just right.

The sun waves back, a playful friend,
Sparrows chirp jokes that never end.
With each giggle, the flowers grow,
And the world spins on in a brightly colored show.

So gather your dreams and let them soar,
In this silly space, you'll never be bored.
For where wishes bloom, joy is the theme,
In the garden of laughter, we all dare to dream.

Tides of Serenity

Waves of laughter wash ashore,
With jellyfish dancing, oh what a score!
Flip-flops giggle as they skip on the sand,
While ice cream cones play in the band.

Each tide pulls in a silly surprise,
Like sunglasses on dogs, and fish in disguise.
Seagulls gossip about the fishy parade,
As sandcastles rise in a playful charade.

A surfboard laughs at the crab's little scuttle,
While seashells whisper, "Let's have a cuddle!"
With a wink from the ocean, we dive in deep,
In this tide of fun, there's no time for sleep.

So ride the waves of joy and delight,
In a sea of chuckles and stars shining bright.
For in this watery world, the heart feels free,
As we sail on waves of silliness and glee.

Safe Harbor of the Heart

In the harbor, where giggles dock,
Soft whispers of joy make the clock mock.
A parrot sings with a wobbly tune,
As treasure chests open to glittering swoon.

Sailboats painted in colors so wild,
Bring stories of fun, oh how they've compiled!
With a wave and a wink, they anchor in place,
Creating a hub for a silly race.

The lighthouse beams with a chuckling glow,
Guiding lost thoughts toward humor's flow.
With each crashing wave, a new joke appears,
As marshmallow clouds drift through laughter's cheers.

So find your harbor where hearts can laugh,
A place for the jolly, a funny photograph.
For in this safe space, we hold and we share,
The joy of connection, the magic of care.

Serene Reflections

In my backyard, a pond of dreams,
Frogs wear crowns, or so it seems.
A picnic spread with ants on guard,
Who knew my lunch would be this hard?

Sunshine dances on my nose,
While squirrels plot in their little clothes.
My hammock swings with giggles loud,
I'm the queen of this tiny crowd.

Clouds parade with shapes so wild,
A giraffe, they claim, but just a child.
With lemonade and silly songs,
Here, nothing ever feels quite wrong.

In a world that's truly mine,
Even chaos feels divine.
So grab a seat, just come on by,
Join the laughter, oh my, oh my!

Haven of Wishes

A treehouse built from dreams of yore,
Where pirates plan and raccoons score.
With cookies baked that look like pie,
A bear's surprise, no one knows why!

Swinging high, I touch the sky,
While butterflies giggle as they fly.
My garden grows with weeds as friends,
Each bloom a giggle that never ends.

A fountain flows with fizzy drinks,
Where laughter bubbles, just think, just think!
With silly hats and socks askew,
In this land, there's always room for you.

So join the fun, let worries wane,
Where joy and laughter dance like rain.
This land of silly never fades,
In this haven, we make parades!

The Garden Within

In my garden, herbs hold secrets tight,
Carrots gossip, taking flight.
Tomatoes blush in shades of red,
While zucchinis play hide-and-seek instead.

Bumblebees dance like they've lost their beat,
While daisies giggle at my bare feet.
I tripped on thyme, fell on a rose,
Now my face is a garden that grows.

Squirrels hold debates on whom to tease,
While sunlight plays tricks with a gentle breeze.
Each petal sings a silly tune,
Laughter blooms beneath the moon.

So come explore this patch of gold,
With every whim and story told.
Among the petals, feel the cheer,
In this garden, joy is near!

Utopia Found

In a land where socks can always pair,
And every fruit's a cozy chair.
Ice cream flows from friendlier skies,
Where every bite brings giggling sighs.

Jellybeans bounce with charm galore,
While lollipops dance on every floor.
Puppies wear capes, cats wear hats,
And everyone chats with friendly spats.

Rainbows drizzle the colors of fun,
Where every race is a silly run.
Each day a party, never a frown,
In this land, we're the talk of the town!

So take my hand, let's skip away,
To this world where we always play.
Fun's the rule, and joy is found,
Oh, what a life, so unbound!

The Cloister of Gentle Breezes

In a garden where socks always vanish,
Lemonade flows like rivers, don't take it for granted.
The squirrels hold court with a peanut decree,
And dance on the lawn with grand jubilee.

Worms wear top hats, peering so proud,
While daisies sway gently, a whole blooming crowd.
Butterflies give talks on how to float,
As bees play the drums on a sweet honeyboat.

A hammock swings low and invites every fool,
To nap 'til they look like a sun-stoked pool.
In this silly retreat with a whimsical spin,
You'll grin at the antics, let the laughter begin.

With each breeze that chuckles, you'll know you belong,
In this funny abode where the world's gone all wrong.
So kick off those shoes and dance 'round the trees,
Welcome to whimsy, where life feels like breeze.

Rays from a Hidden Sun

Underneath clouds that giggle and tease,
We find shining rays that aim to please.
Jellybeans grow beneath a candy floss sky,
As marshmallow clouds huddle ever so shy.

The sun, a trickster, plays peek-a-boo bright,
While shadows make shapes like a kite in flight.
Sunscreen is optional, just cover your toes,
With laughter as lotion, see how it glows!

A parade of odd critters prance down the lane,
With flamingo hats adding style to their game.
Each ray of gumdrops catches silly sights,
While unicorns gallop in rainbow delights.

In this cheerful weirdness, we take our stand,
Where the sunlight's a joke and the world's just as planned.
So let your heart soar, let your joy run,
In a place where laughter is always the sun.

The Nest of Wayward Souls

In a cozy nook where misfits do roam,
Life's more like a circus than a nice, quiet home.
Chickens in bowties squawk tales so grand,
While rabbits in top hats wave their magic hand.

W lamps flicker like stars in a comic book scene,
Where pancakes debate if syrup's the queen.
A cat with a mustache, oh what a sight,
Plays chess with a mouse, oh the sheer delight!

Jokes fly like kites in this whimsical bay,
Each quip, a feather, to lighten the day.
Come join the fun, the games that ensue,
In a nest full of laughter, there's always room for you.

So gather your quirks and let kindness unfold,
In this nest of delights where stories are told.
For in this wild space, you'll surely find,
That laughter's the treasure, a true state of mind.

Sanctuary of the Heart

In this nook where giggles never depart,
Twirling dreams dance, a whimsical art.
With high-flying chairs and upside-down fun,
All the serious faces just come undone.

Walls are adorned with nonsensical quotes,
As flowers wear glasses and sway like old goats.
Each tickling breeze carries stories of laughter,
Of ducks in top hats and their bold haphazard.

A sofa sings ballads when no one is near,
While the fridge tells secrets, enough to bring cheer.
Here, the time stretches like taffy in sun,
A sanctuary blooming for everyone.

So step through the door, leave your woes at the gate,
For in this fair haven, all misfits create.
With hearts made of giggles and whims that ignite,
Embrace the joy within, for it feels just right.

Dreams of Eden

In the garden, laughs abound,
Silly creatures prance around.
Banana peels lay on the ground,
Watch your step; it's joy we've found.

A squirrel juggles pine cones, too,
While giggling frogs sing out their cue.
Sunshine tickles every hue,
In this land, dreams come true.

Mango trees wear frilly hats,
Chasing squirrels play with bats.
Dancing bees wear tiny spats,
Oh, what fun—imagine that!

The moon's a pie, oh what a sight,
Baked just right for starry night.
With whipped cream clouds, what a delight,
In dreams of Eden, all feels right.

Whispers of Tranquility

Down by the stream, fish wear bows,
They swim around with graceful prose.
Ticklish reeds in gentle rows,
Whisper secrets, maybe prose.

Grasshoppers strum on ukuleles,
Squirrels hold nuts like dear old melees.
Birds share jokes, quite funny tales,
While butterflies float, sipping ales.

Even daisies giggle and sway,
They throw a party every day.
The sunbeam dances; come what may,
In this silliness, we wish to stay.

Ripples laugh as they glide by,
Wishing woolly clouds could fly.
Underneath this wide, blue sky,
Tranquility sings—a joyful lie.

Sanctuary of the Heart

In a cozy nook, with socks that clash,
Lies a secret filled with sass.
Here, jellybeans play dress-up, flash,
Dancing about in a sugar smash.

Pillows are clouds; they puff and joke,
Why did the chicken? Oh, what a poke!
Bubble gum hangs, a perfect spoke,
In this heart, no worries evoke.

Furniture hums a cheerful tune,
While the clock moves like a cartoon.
Spilled soup? Just a spoon's buffoon,
We laugh it off; there's no festoon!

An embrace of warmth, soft and bright,
Makes giggles echo through the night.
Sanctuary here, pure delight,
Where laughter reigns, our greatest rite.

Oasis of Solitude

In a hammock tied between two trees,
Sit sipping smoothies with honeybees.
When coconuts fall with a clatter,
Oh, what fun, and do shout, 'Batter!'

Footprints in sand make silly trails,
Where wiggly worms tell funny tales.
Doodles in the skies like sails,
In solitude, laughter never fails.

Pineapples wear sunglasses cool,
As flocks of flamingos play in the pool.
Resting here, we've made a rule,
Self-made giggles are our fuel.

Stars peek down to join the cheer,
Hoping we stay forever near.
An oasis bright, where hearts adhere,
Solitude, yes, but laughter's here!

Abode of Dreams

In a house made of candy, oh what a delight,
With walls of chocolate and rooms full of bright.
Gummy bears dance on a jellybean floor,
While licorice curtains swing open the door.

A garden of lollipops, tall as can be,
Popsicle fountains, it's fun just to see.
Ice cream on rooftops, a sweet; oh dear!
Where every bite whispers, 'Stay, linger here!'

In this goofy domain, where laughter runs free,
Sleepless, for giggles and glee make a spree.
A snooze with some marshmallows right on your head,
Pillow fights lead to the silliest thread.

So pack up your troubles, forget all your woes,
Join in the fun where the cupcake rainbows.
Here dreams take the form of absurd, happy schemes,
In the house that is bursting with candy-coated dreams.

Your Own Horizon

At the edge of the world, with flip-flops and sun,
There's a spot where you sit, a bright place to run.
With seagulls as DJs, they spin salty tunes,
While sandcastles rise up like whimsical moons.

The surf has a joke, it splashes with glee,
Tickling your toes, what a comical spree!
Crabs in the sand wear top hats and ties,
While dolphins juggle fish in their underwater skies.

The sun winks at you, a cheeky old star,
As laughter erupts from a nearby bazaar.
With coconut drinks and umbrellas so bright,
You dance with the wind under stars, oh so light.

So grab your balloon that's as big as your dreams,
And float on the breeze, where fun never seems.
The horizon beckons, with chuckles and zest,
In this place of pure joy, you'll feel truly blessed.

The Heart's Oasis

In a place where the ducks wear hats made of gold,
Palm trees gossip, their stories retold.
The sun sips a drink while the breeze pulls a chair,
And the clouds play hide and seek with the air.

A hammock made of jellybeans sways in the breeze,
Where butterflies chuckle and giggle with ease.
Here every sip of coconut makes you quite sweet,
And rubber ducks gather for a band in the heat.

With sand as soft as marshmallow fluff,
And giggles galore, never too much stuff.
Each sunset bursts colors like crayons let loose,
As the stars start to giggle, a starlit recluse.

So bring your wild heart, your wittiest hat,
In this whimsical spot, where nothing's quite flat.
You'll find all the joy wrapped up in a bow,
In an oasis of laughter where the silliness flows.

Boundless Escape

On a cloud made of pillows, where giggles abound,
You stretch out your limbs on soft, fluffy ground.
With rainbows and unicorns dancing around,
In this place where the silly is the only sound.

The trees wear pajamas and slippers of blue,
And there's ice cream for breakfast, why not, it's true?
The moon is a jester, making mischief at night,
While stars hold a carnival, oh what a sight!

Escape from the dull, step into this cheer,
Where the world is a circus, with joy and good beer.
Juggling your worries, you'll flip them away,
In the landscape of laughter, let's frolic and play.

So pack up your laughter, let's head for the fun,
In a place where the curiosity's never outdone.
With the spirit of whimsy and dreams in your grasp,
You'll find boundless escape in the giggles you clasp.

Celestial Retreats

In a world made of jelly, all sticky and sweet,
One bounces on clouds, oh what a treat!
With sprinkles for raindrops and marshmallow skies,
We giggle through bubbles, where laughter defies.

A place where the chairs wear bright polka dot clothes,
And the squirrels tell secrets while playing with doze.
Here unicorns dance on the soft carpet grass,
Each moment a treasure, let worries bypass.

With ice cream sundaes that float up so high,
We leap like kangaroos as the seagulls fly.
A carnival party, where dreams all collide,
Bright colors and joy forever abide.

So pack up your jokes and your giggles galore,
We'll frolic 'til twilight, then laugh some much more.
In this wacky land where the fairies all cheer,
Life's just a carnival, full of good cheer.

The Dreamer's Cove

Down by the water where the fish wear a tie,
I find pears that giggle and waves that comply.
The turtles tell riddles, the dolphins make jokes,
While bananas serenade the nearby oak folk.

We build sandcastles made of whipped cream delight,
And decorate seashells with glittery light.
The crabs throw a party, they dance in a line,
With jelly beans in hand, they all feel divine.

Clouds fluff like pillows, soft laughs in the breeze,
Dancing in flip-flops, we shimmy with ease.
With every splash, we unleash our great cheer,
In this quirky cove, joy's always quite near.

So come join the fun where the sunsets are dreams,
In a world full of chuckles and sunshine that beams.
Laughter's the compass that guides us away,
To the land where the silliness loves to play.

Whispered Horizons

Upon a horizon where jellybeans grow,
The fish wear tuxedos, swimming to and fro.
If you listen real close, you'll hear the sun giggle,
While the shadows perform their own quirky wiggle.

With pillows for clouds, we drift through the day,
In a carnival garden where silliness sways.
Each flower is singing a jolly old tune,
As the breeze brings a melody, sweet as a swoon.

The hills roll like laughter, alive with the fun,
Where the tickles of breezes run wild in the sun.
We picnic on laughter, sip giggles and glee,
Wandering through spaces, just you and me.

So join in the frolic, let your heart take flight,
In this realm of whimsy, everything feels right.
Where wishes are whispers, and happiness flows,
In a world of pure joy, love constantly grows.

Patterns of Peace

In a land of chortles, where ice cream's the norm,
Where pancakes are flying, all fluffy and warm.
The clocks melt like butter, they giggle and twirl,
In this spot of delight, life's a marvelous swirl.

Here, yodeling llamas lead dances of cheer,
While jelly-fish waltz, spreading joy far and near.
The paintbrush of whimsy draws love in the sky,
As rainbows erupt, we cannot deny.

With daisies in top hats and turtles that spin,
We laugh as we journey, where silliness wins.
A quilt made of giggles, stitched close to our hearts,
Embracing the laughter where bliss never parts.

So join in the revel, let your spirit shine,
In this fabric of joy, our souls intertwine.
In a world full of chuckles, where happiness stays,
We count our bright blessings in zingy displays.

Breath of Bliss

In a land where socks don't match,
And ice cream flows like rivers,
The sun wears shades, it's quite a catch,
While birds wear hats and quiver.

A breeze of laughter fills the air,
As cats in suits debate with dogs,
A dance of silliness and flair,
While frogs read books and drink with frogs.

Forget your worries, leave them here,
On skies of cotton candy skies,
The clouds all whisper, 'Have no fear!'
As elephants wear butterfly ties.

So come and play in fields of glee,
Where jellybeans grow on trees,
And everything is wild and free,
Just like the dance of bumblebees.

Nest of Serenity

In a treehouse made of candy canes,
With gummy bears as loyal friends,
No traffic jams, no workday pains,
    Just fun that never, ever ends.

The squirrels wear ties, oh what a sight,
While birds recite their silly rhymes,
The sun sets slow, with colors bright,
As laughter rings through happy chimes.

A hammock made of licorice strings,
Swaying gently, soft and sweet,
Where giggles dance on angels' wings,
And chocolate rivers kiss your feet.

So find your joy, let worries fly,
On rainbow slides we'll take a ride,
In this sweet nest up in the sky,
Where smiles bloom and dreams abide.

Mythical Shores

On shores of jelly, soft and bright,
The sandcastles smile back at you,
Seagulls wear shades, oh what a sight,
As waves hum tunes and dance for two.

Mermaids juggle, oh what a show,
While dolphins play their ukuleles,
The sunsets glow in a wild woe,
As surfboards ride the taffy swelly.

The crab in a tux invites you near,
While clam shells whisper secrets, bold,
In a world of magic, free of fear,
Where happiness can never grow old.

So splash in colors, bold and bright,
On shores that tickle toes with glee,
Live each day like a delight,
In a realm where you can just be free.

Silence of the Soul

In a spot where giggles never fade,
And the stars wear smiles at night,
A frog plays chess with a lemonade,
While dreams take wing and take flight.

A path of marshmallows leads the way,
Where whispers of humor fill the air,
The moon is cheeky, come what may,
As friendships blossom everywhere.

In this stillness, laughter reigns,
With moments wrapped in silly bows,
Where peace and humor break the chains,
And joy is free, as everyone knows.

So settle in, find your own beat,
In this world of giggles and dreams,
Let your heart dance, let your soul greet,
The funny side of life, it seems.

Your Secret Refuge

In a cozy nook filled with snacks,
Where the phone never rings, and there are no hacks.
With a blanket of chips and soda so bright,
I laugh at the world, what a glorious sight!

The cat's my advisor, judging my choice,
As I binge on the couch, not a care, just rejoice.
My friends are on screens, their laughter feels near,
But here in my hideout, all's festive and clear!

The door is a fortress, it keeps out the gloom,
Outside is for work; in here is for zoom.
With pillows for company, we dance and we sing,
In this magical lair, I am so much a king!

So if you need joy, or a chuckle or two,
Join me in my refuge, we'll make it brand new!
We'll savor the moments, in our little dome,
In this secret retreat, we can always feel home!

The Land of Longing

Somewhere beyond the out-of-reach,
Is a land where I don't have to teach.
With unicorns prancing, creating a song,
Where homework and chores can never go wrong!

Ice cream fountains flow, in flavors galore,
With chocolate chip trees lining every shore.
No alarm clocks allowed, just giggles and play,
In this joyous territory, I'll choose to stay!

The sun wears a hat, all funky and fun,
While rainbows become slides, we take one by one.
With laughter and puzzles spread all around,
In this whimsical space, pure joy can be found!

So come on, dear friend, let's pack up our minds,
And travel through laughter, with no ties that bind.
In this land of longing, we'll frolic with glee,
Living each moment, just you and me!

Canvas of Your Dreams

In a world of colors that never get old,
Each brush stroke whispers a story untold.
With polka-dotted clouds in a pastel sky,
And splashy suns smiling as they float by.

Unicorns skate on rainbows of cheese,
With jellybean flowers, oh please, oh please!
Each corner of dreams, a tickle of cheer,
Where laughter can echo, so loud and sincere!

Painted deserts dance with a sprinkle of fun,
As we swirl through the colors; oh what a run!
Giggling at shadows that bounce in delight,
In this canvas of dreams, everything feels right!

So let's grab our pictures and color the day,
With brushes of joy, in this splendid ballet.
In a whimsical gallery, we'll sparkle and beam,
Creating our masterpiece, chasing each dream!

Hidden Arcadia

In a grove where giggles grow tall as the trees,
And laughter is free, carried softly by breeze.
With squirrels in tuxedos holding high tea,
They insist I sit down, just listen to me!

With secrets so bright, like stars in the night,
I dance with the daisies, what a jovial sight.
Jumping over puddles filled with fizzy pop,
In my hidden arcadia, the fun shouldn't stop!

The grass tickles toes, in a playful embrace,
While butterflies twirl, keeping up with the pace.
In this land of delight, I'll never go back,
For every moment here is joy on the track!

So if you look hard, you might find the key,
To this hidden enclave, come visit with me.
We'll run with the kittens, and dance in the sun,
In our slice of laughter, we'll always have fun!

The Garden of Untamed Wishes

In a patch of grass, a gnome stands tall,
His hat is crooked, he's having a ball.
With daisies talking, and weeds that giggle,
He whispers secrets that make us wiggle.

A snail in a race, just took off his shell,
He claims he's the fastest; we laugh, oh so well.
The flowers dance wildly, the sun starts to grin,
Who knew that a garden could get so much spin?

The worms throw a party, it's quite the charade,
In dirt-clad tuxedos, they're all dressed up made.
Even the roots, they wiggle with flair,
Cheering their friends, all without a care.

In this wild utopia, all dreams are so silly,
Where frogs wear top hats and say, "Aren't we frilly?"
Each wish is a punchline, just waiting to bloom,
In the garden of giggles, there's always more room.

Elysium Beneath the Stars

Under night's blanket, the stars start to snore,
They giggle and twinkle; who could ask for more?
A raccoon in pajamas, he's out for a stroll,
While owls gossip softly, the skies are their role.

Lovebirds are blushing, they've just lost a bet,
With a dance on the grass, it's a scene hard to fret.
A firefly disco with lights in full swing,
Flashing 'round like it's the world's wackiest fling.

A comet's a jester, with jokes on the fly,
While crickets play music, they're never shy.
The moon's just a spotlight, shining so bright,
As laughter erupts, it's pure comic delight.

So join in the laughter, let worries all fade,
In this land of the night, watch the fun parade.
With friends made of stardust, shout cheers to the skies,
In this cheeky wonder, joy never denies!

A Reverie in the Quiet Woods

In the woods so wide, where the squirrels unite,
They're plotting their mischief, ready to blight.
A bear on a bike, oh what a fine sight,
Pedaling slowly, with pure delight.

The trees gather 'round, for a tale full of jest,
Of a fox wearing glasses, who thinks he's the best.
The mushrooms are chuckling, their caps in a twist,
As the raccoons pipe up, "Hey, we can't be missed!"

A parade of odd critters, in marbles and hats,
They'll dance through the glen, like the silliest bats.
A deer prances by, with a colorful bow,
"Watch me twirl!" he shouts, "Come join the show!"

The laughter triggers, a chorus of trees,
In a hum of delight, on the whimsical breeze.
In these woods of wonder, each moment's a gift,
With giggles and grins, laughter starts to uplift.

The Oasis of Forgotten Time

In a bubble of sand, where the camels all lounge,
A parrot tells stories, while sipping a frown.
With dates acting quirky, they roll with a yell,
In this goofy oasis, all's strangely swell.

A cactus with glasses, he's inventing a game,
"Let's play leapfrog, but without any fame!"
The lizards are laughing, their tails in a twist,
As they hop on the boulders, they tumble and list.

A mirage is giggling, it plays hide and seek,
While palm trees hat dance, they're quite the unique.
With coconuts laughing, an uproar we find,
This oasis of whimsy, is one of a kind.

So join in the fun, let time slip away,
With these quirky pals, you'll laugh every day.
In this hidden retreat, where joy holds its reign,
Life's a whimsical ride, like an endless champagne!

Hidden Shores of Serendipity

On beaches made of jelly beans,
Where seagulls sing in silly scenes,
I built a castle with my shoes,
And wore a crown of fruit juice ooze.

The waves bring laughter, not a care,
My surfboard's just a fluffy chair,
The sun's a giant, smiling peach,
I wave to crabs who dance and breach.

Palm trees wear socks, it's quite a sight,
While coconuts race, oh what a plight!
Alligators in sunglasses chill,
Eating tacos upon the hill.

So here's to shores where chuckles reign,
Where every drop of rain is champagne,
This funny place, a land of cheer,
In hidden waves, my joy is clear.

A Realm Crafted by Hope

In gardens where the gnomes run free,
They host a dance with bumblebees,
Where flowers bloom in socks and hats,
And squirrels wear ties, oh fancy chaps.

The trees all giggle, bark and sway,
In shades of blue, they laugh all day,
With lemonade that sprinkles cheer,
We toast to dreams with goofy jeers.

A rainbow slide leads to the moon,
Where marshmallow clouds hum a tune,
While stars play hopscotch, what a show!
In this bright realm, the fun will grow.

With silly signs that point to fun,
Where every race is just a run,
In a crafted place where dreams can pop,
I find my heart will never stop.

Echoes of a Dreamer's Retreat

In a land where dreams are dressed to impress,
Cactus wear suits, oh what a mess!
Floating on pillows, we laugh and roll,
With cupcakes that twirl, they take control.

The rivers run chocolate, oh so divine,
With spry little frogs sipping on wine,
A disco ball hangs from a bright tree,
While owls in tuxedos dance carefreely.

Each corner whispers a roasting joke,
As turtles play poker 'neath the oak,
Dreamers gather, tossing their fears,
In this retreat, we shed our tears.

So let the echoes bring us delight,
In a dreamer's realm, all feels just right,
With laughter and quirks in every nook,
This retreat's a lively storybook.

The Hearth of Unseen Joy

In a cozy nook where socks are friends,
They host a party that never ends,
With mugs of cocoa that giggle and sway,
While marshmallows jam to tunes all day.

The wallflowers bounce like kangaroos,
While curtains shimmy in polka-dot hues,
Fireflies wink as they share their light,
Guiding lost socks through the warm night.

A cat in a bowtie serves up cheese,
While wizards play chess with bumblebees,
In every corner, a secret surprise,
A tickle from laughter, oh how it flies!

So gather around this hearth of cheer,
Where every moment is bright and clear,
In this unseen joy, we laugh and play,
Creating memories that never decay.

www.ingramcontent.com/pod-product-compliance
Lightning Source LLC
Chambersburg PA
CBHW072123070526
44585CB00016B/1539